The Vigyaved Superconsciousness

Ancient Wisdom, Modern Science.

Dr. Yashendra Sethi

i

Copyright © 2024 Dr. Yashendra Sethi

All Rights Reserved.

This book has been self-published with all reasonable efforts taken to make the material error-free by the author. No part of this book shall be used, reproduced in any manner whatsoever without written permission from the author, except in the case of brief quotations embodied in critical articles and reviews.

The Author of this book is solely responsible and liable for its content including but not limited to the views, representations, descriptions, statements, information, opinions and references ["Content"]. The Content of this book shall not constitute or be construed or deemed to reflect the opinion or expression of the Publisher or Editor. Neither the Publisher nor Editor endorse or approve the Content of this book or guarantee the reliability, accuracy or completeness of the Content published herein and do not make any representations or warranties of any kind, express or implied, including but not limited to the implied warranties of merchantability, fitness for a particular purpose. The Publisher and Editor shall not be liable whatsoever for any errors, omissions, whether such errors or omissions result from negligence, accident, or any other cause or claims for loss or damages of any kind, including without limitation, indirect or consequential loss or damage arising out of use, inability to use, or about the reliability, accuracy or sufficiency of the information contained in this book.

Made with ♥ on the Notion Press Platform

www.notionpress.com

About the author

Dr. Yashendra Sethi is a distinguished medical doctor, researcher, and futurist with an insatiable curiosity for the intersections of science, consciousness, and ancient wisdom. He serves as an editor for five major medical journals and as a reviewer for numerous esteemed international publications. With over 100 indexed academic publications to his credit, Dr. Sethi has made significant contributions across diverse fields, including medicine, cardiology, cardio-metabolics, precision medicine, artificial intelligence, computational cardiology, and environmental medicine.

CONTENTS

Beyond his rigorous scientific endeavors, Dr. Sethi identifies as a proud *Sanatani* Hindu — a seeker deeply inspired by the profound truths enshrined in ancient Indian scriptures. For him, these sacred texts are not just relics of history but timeless reservoirs of wisdom that align seamlessly with modern scientific research. Possessing a scientifically inclined and critically questioning mind, he has always admired the harmony between ancient knowledge and the ever-expanding frontiers of contemporary research.

This collection of poems, *The VigyaVed Superconsciousness*, represents an intellectual odyssey — one that invites readers to step beyond conventional thinking and embrace the unknown. Dr. Sethi offers reflections that challenge widely accepted definitions, explore the gaps between science and metaphysics, and weave modern understanding with ancient perspectives. However, these works are not intended as rigid conclusions but as sparks for deeper contemplation, critical thought, and self-discovery.

The author humbly acknowledges that some ideas expressed in this collection may seem unconventional or extend beyond commonly held beliefs. This work is, at its heart, an artistic and intellectual exploration meant for leisure reading, reflection, and inquiry. Readers are encouraged to approach it with an open mind and a spirit of curiosity.

The views and ideas expressed in this book are Dr. Sethi's personal intellectual interpretations and should not be construed as representative of any institution or organization with which he is affiliated. With this offering, he hopes to inspire readers to think critically, ask deeper questions, and embark on their own journeys toward understanding the vast and wondrous nature of existence.

CONTENTS

To my parents, whose unwavering belief in the power of critical thinking and intellectual curiosity has always inspired me to question, explore, and transcend conventional boundaries. You taught me to see beyond the limitations of society, to embrace the unknown, and to fearlessly pursue truth in all its forms. Your wisdom has been the guiding light in my journey to write this collection, reminding me always that true growth lies in looking beyond what is accepted and venturing into realms yet undiscovered.

This book is dedicated to you, with deep gratitude and love.

Contents

CONTENTS

Foreword

In the vast tapestry of human experience, the quest for understanding the nature of consciousness has been one of our most profound and enduring pursuits. Across centuries, from the sacred texts of ancient civilizations to the cutting-edge discoveries of modern science, the journey to uncover the mysteries of the mind, the universe, and the self has revealed both the depth of human curiosity and the limits of our current knowledge.

The VigyaVed Superconsciousness is a beautiful and audacious attempt to bridge this gap, offering a synthesis between ancient wisdom, modern science, and the transformative power of spiritual poetry. Through 108 carefully crafted poems, this collection invites readers into a realm where science and spirituality meet, where the eternal truths of the universe are explored through the lens of both intellect and intuition.

It is rare to encounter a work that so successfully melds these two realms — the rational and the mystical — creating a harmonious space where they not only coexist but enhance and complement each other. This book challenges us to rethink the boundaries of our understanding and to explore the deeper layers of existence. It is both a scholarly pursuit and a soulful journey, woven together with grace and insight.

I am deeply honored to witness the birth of *The VigyaVed Superconsciousness* and offer this foreword as a celebration of its potential to enlighten, inspire, and provoke meaningful contemplation for all those who seek to unlock the mysteries of the universe.

Dr. NK Sethi

BSc, D. Pharm, BAMS, C. Psyche

Foreword

It's indeed a privilege to write a forward to an anthology and no less for the author, brilliant & many faceted Dr Yashendra Sethi, who champions the cause of modern medicine & therapy with as much ease as he does aesthetics, pioneering newer idiom & content in poetry collated in this collection.

One may hardly miss Dr Sethi's creative prowess & depth of assimilation as he negotiates with exemplary flair themes that crosscut metaphysics, philosophy, religiosity & spirituality.

In his writings, an angst and a pining are palpable—that of a quester, seeker, perhaps of the Absolute, the Truth.

As a teacher of his, yours truly had identified in him a prodigal student with immense promise. He has proved to be more than that, he is a polymath, is poised to break grounds and pioneer unprecedented dimensions in aesthetics, poetry too

I wish the anthology get its due reckoning by the aesthetes & literateurs.

Dr Debabrata Roy, MD

Joint Director, R&D

Ex Pro VC, Ras Bihari Bose Subharti University, Dehradun

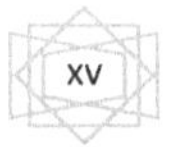

Preface

In the realms of science, philosophy, and spirituality, there exists a timeless question: What is consciousness? Is it merely the product of neural processes, or does it transcend the physical realm, tapping into something far greater? This book, *The VigyaVed Superconsciousness*, emerges from this very inquiry, weaving together the ancient wisdom of the Vedas and Upanishads with the discoveries of modern neuroscience, physics, and consciousness studies.

The collection you hold in your hands is the result of years of introspection, study, and the synthesis of seemingly disparate disciplines. I have sought to capture the essence of both ancient spiritual teachings and contemporary scientific perspectives, crafting a poetic journey that traverses the boundaries of time, space, and knowledge. Each poem represents a step deeper into the understanding of the superconscious mind — that state of awareness beyond the ordinary, where time and space dissolve, and the true nature of the self is revealed. The views expressed herein are my own intellectual interpretations and are not intended to represent any institution, religious doctrine, or definitive scientific truth. I acknowledge that the themes explored may resonate differently with readers depending on their cultural, religious, or scientific backgrounds, and I hope this work fosters a respectful and inclusive dialogue. Please note that scientific concepts are used metaphorically and poetically, rather than as literal explanations, to inspire reflection and inquiry.

Through this book, I hope to inspire readers to reflect on their own understanding of consciousness, to contemplate the unseen forces that shape our lives, and to recognize the interconnectedness of all things. By blending poetry with science and spirituality, *The VigyaVed Superconsciousness* invites you to embark on a transformative journey of self-discovery and enlightenment.

Dr. Yashendra Sethi

Acknowledgments

The completion of this book would not have been possible without the support, guidance, and encouragement of many individuals. I extend my deepest gratitude to the sages and scholars whose wisdom has shaped my understanding of the universe — from the ancient teachings of the Vedas to the breakthroughs of modern science. Their work continues to inspire and inform every word of this collection.

I am also profoundly grateful to my family, friends, and mentors, whose unwavering belief in my vision has sustained me throughout this journey. Their patience and understanding have been invaluable, and their presence in my life is a constant source of strength and inspiration.

I extend my deepest and most heartfelt thanks to my father, Dr. Narendra Kumar Sethi, who has been my greatest motivator and an enduring source of inspiration. His unwavering encouragement to pursue what I love and to think beyond accepted norms has been instrumental in shaping my intellectual journey. Our countless intellectual discussions have fueled my curiosity and critical thinking, guiding me to explore without boundaries.

I also express profound gratitude to my mother, Mrs. Indu Sethi, and my brother, Adv. Jayendra Sethi, who have been a constant source of motivation and support. Their belief in me has been a bedrock of strength throughout this endeavor.

To my teacher, Dr. Debabrata Roy, I offer sincere thanks for instilling in me the powerful belief that "I am no less." Your encouragement has been a guiding light in times of doubt. My teacher and mentor, Dr. Atul Krishnan Bhatnagar, deserves special mention for being a constant inspiration in conscious self-control and mindfulness. His guidance in my journey of meditation has been transformative, helping me deepen my awareness and focus.

I am equally grateful to my teachers: Dr. Nidhi Uniyal, Dr. Ashish Goel, Dr. Arsalan Moinuddin, Dr. Rajesh Tiwari, Dr. Thomas Pavlovic, Dr. Chris Pavlovic, Dr. Gurpreet Johal, & Dr. Sameer Mehta whose kindness and support have been invaluable and who have significantly shaped my clinical and research skills. I also extend thanks to my teachers Dr. Harish Chaturvedi, Dr. Aditi Chaturvedi, and Dr. Bairagi, whose mentorship in both life and work has been a guiding force. Their teachings, especially on breathing techniques for enhanced self-control, have profoundly impacted my personal growth.

To my cherished friends — Dr. Neil Patel, Dr. Nirja Kaka, Dr. Rupal Rai, Dr. Pratik Agarwal, Dr. Vidhi Vora, Dr. Inderbir Padda, Dr. Harsh Shah, Dr, Archi Joshi, Dr. Manjeet Singh Chaudhary, Dr. Esha, Dr. Radhika, Dr. Sonali Dobhal and Dr. Yashveer Chand— I extend my heartfelt gratitude for their unwavering motivation and for constantly championing my academic and non-academic creative work. Your belief in my artistry has encouraged me to embrace and share my passions.

Finally, I extend my heartfelt gratitude to my maasi (maternal aunt), Mrs. Shikha, whose unwavering encouragement inspired me to publish my very first poetry collection, Life - Gusto - Poesy. I am equally thankful to my mama (maternal uncles), Mr. Mintu Chhabra and Mr. Sandeep Chhabra, as well as my cousins, Mr. Anmol Chhabra, and Ms. Divya Chhabra, for their steadfast support in promoting all my extracurricular activities. That humble beginning laid the foundation for this journey, and it is with profound gratitude that I present The VigyaVed Superconsciousness to the world today.

Finally, I would like to express my heartfelt thanks to the readers who will engage with this book. It is for you that these poems were written, and I hope they inspire you to explore the mysteries of existence and the depths of your own consciousness.

Prologue

Consciousness is not a static entity; it is an ever-evolving experience, a constant dance between the known and the unknown. In the world of science, we seek to measure, categorize, and define consciousness, while in the world of spirituality, we explore its boundless nature through meditation, introspection, and self-awareness. *The VigyaVed Superconsciousness* is a bridge between these two worlds — where the meticulous inquiry of science meets the timeless wisdom of the Vedas.

At its core, this book explores the concept of superconsciousness, a state of awareness that transcends the limitations of our everyday minds. This is a consciousness unbound by time, space, or the constraints of the material world. In this state, we access the deepest layers of the self, where our understanding of reality and existence becomes limitless.

The 108 poems within these pages are not just expressions of poetic beauty, but portals to a deeper understanding of the universe and our place within it. They draw on the insights of physics, metaphysics, medicine, neuroscience, and the sacred texts of the ancient world, offering a multifaceted exploration of the nature of consciousness. Each poem is an invitation to look beyond the surface and question the very fabric of reality.

As you journey through these pages, I invite you to let go of preconceptions, to open your mind and heart to new possibilities, and to contemplate the uncharted territories of existence. Through this collection, may you come closer to the truth of who you are and the vastness of the universe that resides within and around you.

1

The Eternal Lattice

In spacetime's weave, where truth aligns,
No present holds, no past confines.
A block eternal, frozen, whole,
Yet Consciousness projects its role,
Collapsing realms, unseen, unknown,
The infinite speaks, yet stands alone.

Entanglement mocks the space between,
A link unseen, yet all-knowing, keen.
Particles bound, though far they lie,
A signalless truth no speed can defy.
Nonlocal whispers, transcendent design,
A cosmos connected, by threads divine.

Relativity bends as light recedes,
Dilating time where velocity leads.
An astronaut sees millennia decay,
While Earth-bound clocks tick slower away.
The frame we hold, the truths we glean,
All shift in the dance of the unforeseen.

Beneath the strings, the manifold hums,
Vibrations where all existence comes.
Dimensions ten, unseen, enshrined,
Where physics unites the concealed with defined.
Our universe, vast, yet a shadow remains,
Holograms trace its cosmic terrains.

The Many Worlds, a branching stream,
Each choice birthing a divergent scheme.
Decoherence casts its dividing hand,
Infinite outcomes through spacetime expand.
Reality fractures, yet Consciousness sees,
Observes the forest while counting the trees.

Entropy, the arrow we trust,
Unfolds in decay, yet hides what's just.
Symmetry waits in a timeless dance,
Where chaos conceals a second chance.
The future flows, rewrites the past,
A temporal loop that forever lasts.

In the holographic bounds of reality's face,
Three dimensions conceal a higher grace.
Encoded truths in planar form,
Project the universe where forces storm.
The observer gazes, the image bends,
Where boundaries blur, and illusion ends.

So stands the lattice, profound, complete,
Where past and future eternally meet.
Pure Consciousness, the primal law,

The fabric of being, the cosmic awe.
A paradox reigns in this infinite tale,
Timeless, unbroken—a truth unveiled.

2

The Observer's Paradox

Unseen, the observer shapes the frame,
Reality bends at consciousness' name.
A wave but whispers until gazed upon,
Its being arising as presence is drawn.
What was potential becomes the real,
Measured and marked by the mind's ideal.

Yet who is the seer that holds such might?
Where do they dwell—beyond or in sight?
Bound to the body, or free of its cage,
A timeless entity, neither young nor age.
It peers through the veil of matter's disguise,
A truth beyond the material skies.

Here lies the paradox, vast and profound,
Where presence shapes what spacetime has bound.
The cosmos unfolds as an endless decree,
Yet it arises only for eyes that see.
A universe dormant, silent, untamed,
Awakes as the observer calls it named.

3

Entropy's Deception

Time moves forward, unyielding, austere,
An arrow that flies toward chaos severe.
Order dissolves in entropy's sway,
The structures of being destined to decay.
Yet hidden within this apparent demise,
A secret persists, where creation lies.

For what appears broken is often reformed,
Through patterns emerging where chaos has stormed.
The phoenix ascends from entropy's flame,
Life's cycles repeat, yet are never the same.
In ruin is birth, in death is design,
The arrow of time is a line intertwined.

So, entropy dances, its laws misread,
Its march births life where all seemed dead.
The universe swells with ceaseless strife,
Yet in this disorder persists the seed of life.
What perishes reforms, forever concealed,
A truth of renewal that time has revealed.

4

The Holographic Realm

In each atom's core, the cosmos resides,
Its essence reflected, though subtly it hides.
The universe etched on a planar disguise,
Infinite vastness compressed to the wise.
A hologram gleams where dimensions unite,
A secret encoded in the absence of light.

What is projected, and what is real?
A riddle encoded in spacetime's seal.
The vast expanse of stars and stone,
May be shadows cast from the truly known.
Yet even the shadow speaks of the whole,
A vision refracted through the conscious soul.

This holographic truth, a mystic lore,
Links the finite with the infinite's core.
What lies beyond perception's gate,
Speaks not of distance, but of fate.
The cosmos reflects in each point and part,
As infinity folds into the mindful heart.

5

The Entanglement of Souls

Two particles sundered by space and time,
Bound by a bond both sacred and prime.
No signal conveyed, no distance divides,
Yet they whisper across spaceless tides.
Entangled truths in a silent embrace,
Defy the limits of spacetime's trace.

Such too are souls, though distant they seem,
They share a thread from a deeper dream.
Invisible ties that cannot be torn,
Speak of a unity timelessly worn.
The quantum of love, the binding unseen,
Links us all in existence's scheme.

To understand this is to transcend the small,
To see the self in the All and the All.
For particles distant are truly one,
Bound by the light of the same central sun.
Entanglement whispers of unity vast,
An eternal connection, unbroken, steadfast.

6

The Many Worlds Refrain

Each choice we make is a universe born,
A thread of existence, split and adorned.
For every action, a path untold,
A fractal of timelines endlessly rolled.
In branching realities, all paths unfold,
Every "what if" preserved, uncontrolled.

Yet Consciousness stands at a singular gate,
Collapsing potentials into a chosen fate.
It threads through the Many, weaving one line,
Binding the endless to what we define.
Observer and actor, creator and guide,
Consciousness shapes the multiverse wide.

What seems like chaos, the splitting of streams,
Is order concealed in quantum dreams.
Beyond the branches, a unity waits,
The Many converge at infinity's gates.
And through this lens, one truth will shine,
The observer is all, both human and divine.

7

The Illusion of Now

The Now deceives with its fleeting grace,
A moment suspended in time's endless race.
Yet when grasped, it vanishes to the void,
A phantom construct we strive to avoid.
Time flows forward, unyielding, unsound,
Yet all moments converge, eternally bound.

For the present is not what it seems to be,
It folds into past and future's decree.
A unity hidden, where time dissolves,
And the mind's illusion no longer revolves.
To live in the Now is to see it expand,
To embrace the infinite in its transient strand.

Through meditation's gaze, the veils unwind,
The layers of time dissolve in the mind.
The past and future, no longer apart,
Rejoin in the stillness of the conscious heart.
The illusion of Now becomes a doorway vast,
Where all of eternity is held fast.

8

The Silent Singularity

In the singular heart of spacetime's fold,
Lies the infinite, ancient and cold.
No mass, no time, no light can remain,
All that exists, dissolved and contained.
This is the cradle where being will bloom,
A silent singularity, a cosmic womb.

Yet from this void springs the universe wide,
A moment of birth from where laws collide.
All matter and motion, all force and flame,
Emerging unbidden, unbound by name.
The void, a paradox, both fertile and bare,
Holds the essence of all that is there.

What lies at the center of spacetime's clasp?
Not an end, but a question no mind can grasp.
The singularity whispers in infinite tones,
Its silence louder than all we've known.
Creation's source is not what it seems,
An eternal enigma beyond our dreams.

9

Dimensions Unseen

Beyond the three, where the senses reside,
Lie realms of existence the mind must decide.
A fourth emerges, time's steady stream,
Folding moments into a singular dream.
Yet further dimensions, curled and obscure,
Hold secrets the finite cannot endure.

Each plane enfolds a universe wide,
Infinite truths in finite guise hide.
Space bends to shapes no eye can discern,
Geometries infinite for the soul to learn.
As strings vibrate in a cosmic ballet,
Dimensions unseen hold eternity's sway.

The Vedas once whispered of such veils profound,
Of realms where the infinite's echoes resound.
Science now seeks what sages once knew,
Realms interwoven, both many and few.
Dimensions whisper of truths beyond,
Of a unity vast to which all are bound.

10

The Duality of Time

Time's river flows, relentless, austere,
Yet past and future are ever near.
The arrow proceeds, linear, clear,
But hidden cycles circle the sphere.
Time as dual, a paradox vast,
Both fleeting present and eternal past.

Kala, the devourer, consumes all things,
Yet within its grasp, the timeless springs.
In the folds of moments, the eternal hides,
A cyclic rhythm that never subsides.
Vedic hymns speak of time's two faces,
Linear pathways and cyclical traces.

Einstein unveiled time's pliable guise,
Curving with gravity, warping the skies.
But sages knew what physics confirms,
Time is a circle, not merely a term.
Duality reigns in this cosmic play,
Time's truth revealed in the meditative sway.

11

The Singularity of Self

The Self, eternal, neither born nor bound,
In spacetime's web, it cannot be found.
It watches the play of matter and mind,
A silent observer, unshackled, refined.
The cosmos reflects in its infinite gaze,
Yet it stands untouched by spacetime's haze.

Physics seeks origins, the primordial flame,
Yet the Self persists, beyond form and name.
The Upanishads whisper, science confirms,
The observer is key, through all it affirms.
For what is existence, if none perceive?
The Self is the truth we endlessly weave.

Consciousness sits at creation's heart,
The source of the whole, not just a part.
The singularity of being dissolves the divide,
Between observer and observed, the infinite inside.
In meditation, this truth is clear,
The Self is all, both distant and near.

12

The Infinite Recursion

Within the infinite, a fractal unfurls,
Patterns repeating in cosmic swirls.
From atoms to stars, the echoes resound,
A recursion of forms, eternally bound.
The macro in micro, the small in the vast,
A mirror of truths from future to past.

The Upanishads spoke of Brahman's guise,
Reflected in droplets, as oceans arise.
Physics finds echoes in fractal designs,
Where nature repeats in infinite lines.
Each layer a veil, each part a whole,
Each recursion a glimpse of the universal soul.

The universe folds into itself once more,
An endless reflection, a limitless shore.
In meditation's depths, these patterns appear,
A vision of unity, profound and clear.
Infinite recursion in a finite guise,
Speaks of the eternal that never dies.

13

Duality of Light and Shadow

In light's embrace, the cosmos was born,
Yet shadow arises, its presence sworn.
Wave and particle, dual in its state,
A paradox bound to existence's fate.
Light illumines, yet it conceals,
The shadow's truths, which darkness reveals.

The Vedas spoke of the play of the two,
Of Maya's veil and the light piercing through.
Physics reveals what mystics proclaimed,
Light's dual nature, by no path tamed.
Illusion and truth in cosmic dance,
Shadow and light in an eternal romance.

For without the shadow, light is unseen,
The interplay defines what has been.
Meditation bridges the gap of their sway,
Uniting the opposites in a transcendent way.
Light and shadow, both sides of the coin,
In unity's truth, their meanings conjoin.

14

The Harmony of the Five Elements

Earth, water, fire, air, and space,
The building blocks of existence's face.
Solid, fluid, energy's blaze,
Breath and void in cosmic embrace.
Physics speaks of matter's form,
But elements whisper of a unity born.

Pancha Mahabhuta, the sages intoned,
Through them the universe is endlessly honed.
Modern science sees quarks and force,
But Vedic wisdom charts the primal course.
The macro and micro, a harmonious strain,
Matter and spirit in dual refrain.

To know the elements is to bridge the divide,
Between the physical world and the soul inside.
Through meditation, their unity is clear,
Each element sacred, each essence near.
The cosmos sings in their balanced accord,
A hymn to creation, endlessly adored.

15

Beyond the Veil of Perception

The senses deceive, they show but a part,
Of the infinite truths that dwell in the heart.
What we perceive is a fragment confined,
A shadowed echo of the universal mind.
Beyond perception lies realms untold,
Where wisdom ancient and future unfold.

The Vedic seers saw through this veil,
Into dimensions where truths prevail.
Science now peers with its tools refined,
Yet still cannot grasp what lies unaligned.
What is unseen is not absent or void,
But infinite potential yet unalloyed.

To break this veil, one must go within,
Through meditation, the journey begins.
Beyond the senses, the soul takes flight,
To realms of wisdom, to eternal light.
There the untold and unseen reside,
In unity vast, with nothing to divide.

16

The Illusion of Sight

The eyes deceive, though sharp they seem,
A kaleidoscope locked in a limited dream.
Photons strike, but truth refracts,
A distorted image is all it extracts.

Neurons weave what the retina transmits,
Filling voids where detail sits.
Yet the edges blur in a seamless haze,
As the mind reshapes the light it betrays.

Physics whispers of waves and quanta,
Of realities hidden in light's grande casa.
Yet the brain's canvas holds but a part,
A fractal sketch of the cosmos' art.

Our sight is a fragment, a shadow at best,
A window too narrow to see the rest.
Meditate deeper, and you'll find,
Vision beyond the optical bind.

For the universe's truth is far from our gaze,
Unseen in the spectrum our senses appraise.
To see what lies beyond this play,
We must close our eyes and look another way.

17

The Mind's Cage

Trapped in the skull, the mind does dwell,
A prisoner to signals its senses tell.
Electrical currents define what is real,
A chemical orchestra in its ceaseless wheel.

Synaptic bridges and dopamine streams,
Shape our lives and construct our dreams.
Yet beyond these bounds lies a grander scope,
Unshackled truths and infinite hope.

The sages spoke of a mind unbound,
Beyond neurotransmitters and temporal sound.
Modern science edges close to the door,
Yet the infinite lies forevermore.

We chase fleeting pleasures, avoid fleeting pain,
Yet know not the why, nor what we gain.
The brain's own cage keeps reason confined,
While the soul longs for the truths undefined.

Escape this cage, through stillness profound,
Transcend the circuits where thoughts rebound.
There lies freedom, eternal and vast,
Beyond the mind, the truth unsurpassed.

18

Perception's Paradox

What we perceive is a crafted lie,
A neural mirage the world implies.
The brain completes what it cannot see,
Painting a picture from partial debris.

From sounds that echo to shadows cast,
We grasp at illusions, shadows amassed.
Time itself bends to the mental frame,
A subjective puzzle, never the same.

Physics calls it relativistic art,
Where space and time cannot stay apart.
Neurology shows how the brain distorts,
Adjusting reality into mental cohorts.

But beyond the paradox of what we perceive,
Lies a reality we barely believe.
Meditation unveils these layered facades,
Revealing a cosmos that endlessly nods.

For the truth remains ever out of reach,
A horizon of thought no language can teach.
Yet in silent reflection, a glimpse may appear,
Of a truth unbounded, timeless, and clear.

19

The Smallness of Grief

We cry for loss, for wounds that sting,
For fleeting joys the world may bring.
Yet zooming out, the sorrow fades,
A speck of dust in cosmic parades.

Neurology says it's the amygdala's plight,
Anchoring pain to the mind's finite light.
Chemical signals make heartbreak seem,
Larger than life, a consuming stream.

Yet galaxies spin, unbothered, unwound,
Indifferent to pains that humans have found.
Our sadness, though deep, is utterly small,
A whisper lost in the universe's hall.

The sages knew what science now probes,
That pain dissolves when the soul explodes.
Beyond the self, beyond petty care,
Lies a vastness no grief can impair.

To mourn the trivial is to miss the grand,
A cosmos immense, an eternal strand.
Adjust your focus, let sadness dissolve,
In the infinite, all problems resolve.

20

Truth Beyond the Brain

The brain is vast, yet finite in scope,
A biological machine with evolutionary hope.
Its faculties, sharp, yet narrow in range,
Blind to realities distant and strange.

Neurons fire, thoughts arise,
Yet cannot grasp the infinite skies.
For the brain is bound by time and space,
A fleeting observer of the cosmic grace.

Quantum realms defy its grasp,
In nonlocal truths, the mind cannot clasp.
The Upanishads whisper of knowledge unbound,
Where the eternal Self is forever found.

Futurists dream of minds augmented,
Brains rewired, and perception extended.
Yet even in progress, the truth remains,
Beyond the circuits of mortal brains.

To find the truth, go beyond the mind,
To the pure consciousness, timelessly aligned.
Where past, present, and future converge,
In unity vast, all illusions submerge.

21

Consciousness as a Unified Field

The mind perceives, yet knows not how,
A spark within the fleeting Now.
Neurons fire, and thought takes form,
A fragile beacon in the neural storm.

But what connects the thoughts we bear?
What binds our dreams, transcends despair?
Quantum fields speak of entangled might,
Hindu sages saw this as Conscious Light.

No synapse alone can birth the soul,
It is the field that makes us whole.
A cosmic web, beyond the brain,
Where truth and essence ever remain.

The Upanishads called it the Self Divine,
Unchanging, eternal, beyond space and time.
Science falters at this hidden seal,
But Consciousness waits, the Unified Field.

22

The Quantum Mind

Electrons whirl in probabilistic streams,
A quantum ballet, a dance of dreams.
Particles blink in and out of place,
Defying the laws of time and space.

The brain, a quantum machine in disguise,
Processes truths it cannot realize.
Hindu texts spoke of a mind unbound,
Where quantum truths and wisdom are found.

Schrödinger pondered, as sages foretold,
That life is a thread from the cosmos unrolled.
A paradox of form, a wave, a spark,
Light within light, flame in the dark.

Meditate deeply, and you may perceive,
The quantum realm where particles weave.
In stillness, the truth begins to unfurl,
That the mind itself is a quantum world.

23

The Illusion of Linear Time

Time moves forward—or so it seems,
A flowing river of fleeting dreams.
Yet physics whispers another tale,
Of loops and folds where clocks may fail.

Einstein showed that time's a frame,
Relative and fluid, never the same.
Hindu wisdom spoke long before,
Of Kalachakra, the timeless core.

The past and future entwine the now,
A superposition the ancients avow.
Meditation bends this rigid line,
Revealing truths beyond space-time.

In timeless silence, the seeker finds,
The illusions that shackle our mortal minds.
For time itself is but a part,
Of the greater whole, the eternal heart.

24

The Duality of Reality

Waves and particles, two forms, one thing,
A duality Einstein could not bring.
Mind and matter, distinct yet tied,
A cosmic truth science cannot hide.

Advaita spoke of this paradox clear,
That duality reigns in what we hold dear.
Perception splits what is truly one,
A shadow cast by the central sun.

Brain and soul are not apart,
They're facets of a greater heart.
The scientist and mystic must join their art,
To grasp the whole, to know the start.

Meditate deeper, and you will see,
That duality veils the unity free.
For all divides are illusions thin,
The cosmos and self are one within.

25

The Incompleteness of Perception

We see the world through filtered eyes,
A spectrum narrow, a field that lies.
The brain completes what it cannot know,
Filling the gaps in its mental show.

Neurology maps the senses' flight,
But misses the truths beyond its sight.
The Rishis called it Maya's veil,
A web of illusions where seekers fail.

What lies beyond this fractured view?
The infinite vast, the eternal true.
Physics hints, yet cannot display,
The unseen realms where truths hold sway.

To transcend the senses, one must be still,
And see with the eye beyond the will.
For the cosmos is larger than we can perceive,
And greater truths await those who believe.

26

The Brain's Illusion of Self

"I" is a thought the mind constructs,
A fleeting phantom it subtly instructs.
Neurology says it's a neural scheme,
A persistent illusion, a waking dream.

Hindu texts speak of the Atman true,
The unchanging Self beyond the view.
The ego dissolves in meditative light,
Revealing the soul as the cosmos' might.

The brain weaves stories of "me" and "mine,"
But the eternal Self is free of time.
Science and mysticism converge to show,
The illusion of self must let go.

For the truth of who we are runs deep,
Beyond the mind, where the infinite sleeps.
Awake, and know what sages teach,
That the Self is all, and within your reach.

27

The Paradox of Pursuit

In the labyrinth of longing, where reason frays,
Desire forges its most perilous maze.
Each fervent step, a tethered snare,
Binding the seeker in loops of despair.

The prize pursued with relentless zeal,
Turns jagged, refusing its promised appeal.
A home of grandeur, its beams now creak,
The weight of ambition too fragile, too weak.

That love, once craved with unyielding might,
Now casts its shadow, eclipsing delight.
A bauble gleaming in distant repose,
Up close, a reflection of woes it bestows.

Fortune recoils from the overdrawn plea,
A tide that ebbs from a grasping sea.
The more one reaches, the less it remains,
A feast withheld, though hunger sustains.

Abandon the chase, let stillness decide,
For treasures approach when longing subsides.
In seeking too fiercely, one often ensures,
The trouble desired will forever be yours.

28

Dimensions Beyond Sight

We live in three, yet space may hold,
Ten or more, as string theories unfold.
Curled in corners, dimensions unseen,
A cosmic truth, both vast and serene.

Hindu lore speaks of realms profound,
Lokas infinite, where truths abound.
The yogis traveled through inner skies,
To dimensions beyond where physics lies.

Science seeks these hidden planes,
Where gravity dances and logic strains.
Meditation mirrors this quest of old,
Revealing worlds the sages foretold.

Beyond these dimensions, what do we find?
Infinite realities, the eternal mind.
For the cosmos is layered, vast, and grand,
A fractal unfolding at every hand.

29.

The Mechanics

Of Meditation

The brain aligns in rhythmic flow,
Alpha waves in a tranquil glow.
Neurology maps this meditative state,
Where chaos yields to a harmonious fate.

But physics sees a deeper game,
Where consciousness shapes the quantum frame.
The sages said, in meditative trance,
The cosmos itself will join the dance.

The mind, when still, transcends the brain,
Touching the source from which all came.
Science and mysticism converge at last,
To reveal the future, and grasp the past.

Meditation is the portal true,
To dimensions vast and visions new.
For in the silence of the cosmic sea,
Lies the answer to what we seek to be.

30

The Unreachable Truth

What we know is a fleeting thing,
A fragment torn from the infinite string.
The brain constructs, but cannot hold,
The entirety of truths untold.

The Upanishads sing of wisdom pure,
Of a truth beyond what senses assure.
Science probes with a narrow gaze,
Blind to the light of eternal rays.

The sages whispered what physics sees,
That the cosmos hides in mysteries.
No formula grasps the truth complete,
For infinity laughs at our finite feat.

Past, present, future, a single thread,
A tapestry woven where time has fled.
To know the truth, let the self dissolve,
And the eternal mystery shall resolve.

31

The Eternal Now

Beneath the ticking clock's parade,
Where moments pass, yet none are stayed,
Lies a truth no chronicle can bind,
Timelessness etched in the conscious mind.

Advaita whispers, "You are That,"
Beyond the past, where futures sat.
In still awareness, the layers fall,
Revealing a Now that contains it all.

Time's illusion fractures, fades,
A fleeting shadow the ego made.
Wisdom whispers, soft and clear,
Eternity within, drawing near.

The seeker finds in silence deep,
A stillness where no clocks can creep.
Pure Consciousness, the boundless sea,
Unmoved by time's frail decree.

For past and future lose their frame,
When Truth calls forth its timeless name.
And in that moment—free and whole,
One feels eternity within the soul.

32

Time Dissolved in the Infinite

What is time but a fleeting guise,
A veil drawn low across the skies?
The sages saw its fractured art,
An endless stream where none depart.

In meditation, time refrains,
The past and future cease their chains.
Advaita's Truth, unbound, unfolds,
The eternal Now the cosmos holds.

In moments bare, the silence spoke,
Where timeless awareness softly woke.
The clock dissolves, its hands erased,
In the void where presence is embraced.

Physics seeks to measure and bind,
But cannot grasp the timeless mind.
Where waves collapse, and truths collide,
The eternal present cannot hide.

In Pure Consciousness, the seeker learns,
That time is not, yet the soul still yearns.
For past, present, and future combine,
In an infinite Now, the divine design.

33

The Anatomy of Love

In chambers four, the heart resides,
A pump of blood, yet more it hides.
For science sees its rhythmic play,
But cannot measure love's array.

Neurons fire, a spark is born,
Dopamine dances, desires adorn.
Oxytocin flows, the bond is sealed,
In circuits where the soul is revealed.

Yet love's no prisoner of the brain,
It transcends the body's fleeting domain.
An unseen force, profound, divine,
Where flesh and spirit intertwine.

It drives creation, life's design,
From child to parent, a sacred line.
The heart's mere muscle, yet still we feel,
Love's pulse, eternal, strong, and real.

And so, though science probes its art,
Love lingers, vast, within the heart.
A mystery science cannot chart,
The universe's truest part.

34

The Unseen Soul

Eternal, untouched by time's cruel hand,
Love exists, a silent strand.
No birth, no death, no start, no end,
A boundless force, we transcend.

Through endless ages, it remains,
Untouched by loss, beyond all pains.
The body fades, yet love still grows,
A timeless river, it forever flows.

We wear this shell, so frail, so light,
But deep within, love burns bright.
Unseen, unfelt, yet always near,
Love whispers softly, "Do not fear."

Love, like the soul, is ever true,
Beyond the veil, it will renew.
In every heart, it finds its place,
A force of light, an endless grace.

35

Love as a Devotional Flame

Love burns within, a sacred fire,
Igniting the soul, transcending desire.
In devotion's path, the ego fades,
And in the infinite, love cascades.

A silent melody stirs the heart,
A resonance beyond the mind's chart.
Unseen forces weave their art,
Binding the whole to its eternal part.

Reason falters where devotion prevails,
On boundless seas, love sets its sails.
Not born of us, but a cosmic thread,
A force that lives beyond the dead.

To love is prayer, a timeless rite,
A yielding to an endless light.
The self dissolves in this luminous stream,
Where love becomes the eternal dream.

In this surrender, the soul ascends,
Finite forms meet infinite ends.
Love is not emotion, but the way,
To merge with the eternal play.

36

Love Through the Scientific Lens

In labs and studies, graphs and scans,
They map the course of love's demands.
A chemical storm, a neural dance,
A game of chance, biology's trance.

The brain ignites when passions rise,
Electromagnetic storms disguise,
How love's but molecules in flight,
Binding hearts in the day and night.

But science falters, falls apart,
At the sacred mystery of the heart.
For love defies the atom's rule,
Its depth cannot be gauged by tool.

It is the bond that life sustains,
Beyond what matter's form explains.
A force unseen, yet ever near,
The spark that brings existence here.

Love's not confined to neural schemes,
It shatters logic, births our dreams.
A mystery no science solves,
For love is where the cosmos evolves.

37

Vocational Love

To love one's craft, to give one's all,
To heed the sacred, higher call.
The surgeon's hands, the poet's word,
A love for work that's deeply stirred.

It is the teacher shaping minds,
The healer's touch that always binds.
In service lies this truth so vast,
That love for labor can outlast.

This love transcends reward or gain,
It eases toil, it softens pain.
A mission drawn from soul's deep well,
Where purpose and passion forever dwell.

For to create is love's pure art,
To give one's work a beating heart.
Vocational love is life's decree,
A devotion to what's meant to be.

And so, in work, the soul can find,
A love that elevates mankind.
Through purpose, passion, and resolve,
Life's grandest mysteries evolve.

38

Love as the Universal Emotion

Love weaves a thread through every soul,
It binds the parts to form the whole.
In every heart, it makes its mark,
A common flame, a shared spark.

Across the earth, no walls can stand,
Against love's universal command.
It needs no tongue, it speaks in eyes,
In silent whispers, beneath the skies.

Love's not confined by race or creed,
It answers every human need.
A balm for pain, a cure for fear,
A light that makes the darkness clear.

From stranger's smile to mother's care,
Love's presence lingers everywhere.
Its laws are simple, yet profound,
A force eternal, unbound.

It shapes the stars, the earth, the sea,
The grandest truth that sets us free.
For love is life's unbroken thread,
A gift unmeasured, forever spread.

39

The Alchemy of Success

Gold in hand or dream in mind,
Success is crafted, step-defined.
A spark of will, a neuron's fire,
The brain rewires to lift us higher.

Synaptic paths are forged anew,
Habits shaped, intentions true.
Through focus clear, the journey starts,
From thought to deed, the alchemist's art.

Hindu texts whisper ancient lore,
Karma's wheel, dharma's core.
Align your work, surrender gain,
And find true wealth beyond the mundane.

For power sought through ego's game,
Leaves hollow hearts, a fleeting flame.
But power wielded with intent pure,
Becomes a force to heal, endure.

Success is not just what's amassed,
But in each moment fully grasped.
The real treasure, hidden within,
Awaits when outer quests grow thin.

40

Power's Illusion and Truth

Power, they say, corrupts the soul,
Yet sought by all to feel control.
But true strength lies not in command,
But in a heart that understands.

The Bhagavad Gita's timeless phrase,
Speaks of a power that does not faze:
To master self, to still the mind,
Is to hold a force no chains can bind.

Science reveals the brain's design,
Addicted to power's dopamine line.
Yet only when power serves the good,
Can it be rightly understood.

For what is power if not a chance,
To lift another, to advance?
A fleeting king on a fragile throne,
True power lies in the self alone.

And so, the wise seek not control,
But harmony, a balanced role.
Power fades when life is done,
But truth and love outshine the sun.

41

Manifestation: The Mind's Magnet

In realms of thought, where dreams arise,
Manifestation clarifies.
The subconscious shapes the world we see,
A mirror to our energy.

The Vedas teach, and science confirms,
Our minds, like fields, shift life's terms.
Neurons fire, intentions set,
The brain becomes the cosmic net.

But action must with thought combine,
For dreams alone won't make life shine.
Karma calls for deeds aligned,
To make the abstract world refined.

Success blooms where effort meets belief,
And steady hands sow life's relief.
The universe echoes what you give,
Manifesting the way you live.

Yet beware the ego's endless greed,
True wealth is found in meeting need.
For life aligns with pure intent,
When love and service are the rent.

42

The Neuroscience of Achievement

Deep in the cortex, plans unfold,
The brain's a map of stories told.
Each thought, a spark, a pathway traced,
Success rewired, habits replaced.

The prefrontal guides with logic's sway,
While limbic whispers sway our way.
Dopamine's pull, the reward we chase,
Motivation in the neural space.

Yet modern minds are often torn,
By distractions new, ambitions worn.
Meditation stills the racing tide,
Letting focus, like a compass, guide.

Success begins in this rewired art,
To train the brain, to match the heart.
Aligning goals with inner peace,
Unlocks a flow that will not cease.

For achievement's root is balance found,
A steady mind on fertile ground.
And science proves what sages said,
A calm mind keeps the spirit fed.

43

Wealth: Material and Spiritual

Wealth, a mirage, a fleeting shore,
Brings pleasure brief, but nothing more.
The Upanishads reveal its hue,
True wealth is found in wisdom's view.

Physiology craves the stable line,
Shelter, food, the body's shrine.
But beyond the flesh, the soul aspires,
To wealth that lifts, that never tires.

Modern psychiatry maps the toll,
Of wealth pursued without a goal.
Anxieties rise, contentment wanes,
A golden cage for mortal pains.

True riches flow from service deep,
From love you give, not wealth you keep.
The Bhagavad Gita's eternal refrain,
Calls for balance, beyond worldly gain.

For wealth amassed for ego's sake,
Is but a chain we cannot break.
But wealth that serves the greater good,
Turns base desires to sacred wood.

44

The Heart of Fulfillment

Why do we chase what fades away,
While life itself slips day by day?
Hindu wisdom speaks of this flaw,
Maya veils the eternal law.

Success and power, though sweet, deceive,
Their fruits decay, and hearts bereave.
True joy lies in a timeless ground,
Where fleeting cravings are unbound.

Consciousness, the grandest throne,
Holds treasures far beyond the known.
The Upanishads call the seeker's name,
To transcend the ego's fleeting flame.

For fulfillment comes not from more,
But from within, a sacred core.
And those who see past life's charade,
Find the joy that cannot fade.

Thus, wealth and power serve their part,
But cannot fill the yearning heart.
The wise transcend, the soul ascends,
To find a love that never ends.

45

The Shadow of Greed

Greed, a whisper, soft and sly,
Promises much, yet leaves us dry.
In the brain's reward, its seeds are sown,
A cycle spins, a hunger grown.

The amygdala flares, the prefrontal bends,
Logic crumbles, as impulse ascends.
Yet ancient texts forewarned this fate,
Desire unchecked, a closing gate.

From wealth of gold to wealth of thought,
What matters most is seldom sought.
Vedanta guides us to release,
To find in letting go, our peace.

For greed is hunger's hollow mask,
Feeding shadows, an endless task.
But the soul, unbound by grasping hand,
Finds its wealth in the infinite strand.

46

The Neuroscience of Gratitude

Gratitude, the simplest art,
Rewires the mind, renews the heart.
The limbic calms, the prefrontal sings,
The neural gift that balance brings.

MRI scans reveal the glow,
Of thankfulness, where synapses flow.
Endorphins rise, cortisol falls,
Gratitude breaks anxiety's walls.

The Gita speaks of humble grace,
Of finding joy in life's embrace.
To see the sacred in the small,
Is to transcend the ego's call.

For science and spirit here align,
To show the path, the grand design.
A grateful heart, a peaceful mind,
In unity, true wealth we find.

47

Ambition's Dual Edge

Ambition sharpens like a blade,
To carve new paths, yet casts a shade.
For every summit sought and won,
Leaves shadows lengthening with the sun.

The Bhagavad Gita warns the seeker,
Ambition strong can make one weaker.
To act without attachment's bind,
Is the highest freedom for the mind.

The brain, it craves the dopamine,
A fleeting rush, a shallow sheen.
But wisdom whispers in the din,
True joy's not found in what we win.

Ambition balanced, tempered, true,
Transforms what's done, in what we view.
To climb for service, not for pride,
Makes every step a holy stride.

48

The Currency of Meaning

What is wealth if not a story told,
A myth we chase, a dream we hold?
But meaning speaks a richer tone,
A life lived well, not spent alone.

Psychiatry finds the neural thread,
Connection heals where meaning's bred.
The vagus hums, the spirit glows,
When purpose flows where the heart goes.

The ancient texts teach of life's four aims,
Artha, Dharma, with passion flames.
Yet Moksha waits, the final prize,
Beyond the wealth that clouds the skies.

For meaning's currency can't be weighed,
In gold or fame, where fears parade.
It's found in moments deeply sown,
In service true, and seeds we've grown.

Thus wealth, success, and power align,
When tied to purpose, grand, divine.
A life of meaning, rich and vast,
Turns fleeting dreams to truths that last.

49

The Subconscious Vault

In depths unseen, the mind does steer,
A vault of thought, of joy and fear.
The subconscious molds the paths we tread,
A silent guide to where we're led.

Hindu sages long have known,
The seeds within are often sown.
Through mantra, breath, and inward gaze,
They sought to pierce the hidden maze.

Science too now maps this space,
The brain's vast, unseen interface.
Neuroplasticity reshapes the plan,
Unlocking power within the span.

To master self is no small art,
It asks of us a patient heart.
But once unbound, the mind can soar,
To realms of peace, and nothing more.

Thus, wealth of mind precedes all gain,
A power forged not through the vein.
To know the self is to command,
A boundless world within the hand.

50

The Weight of Integrity

A thousand deeds may build a name,
But one misstep can mar its flame.
For character, unseen yet bold,
Outweighs the lure of fleeting gold.

In science as in life's great art,
Integrity forms the beating heart.
Atoms align in patterns true,
Just as actions define what is due.

A fractured bond, a broken trust,
Turns thriving steel to fragile rust.
Yet truth upheld, though trials test,
Shapes the soul into its best.

In every choice, the self is laid,
A sculpture formed by each cascade.
For how we act in quiet halls,
Resounds beyond life's grandest walls.

Hold fast to honor, let it steer,
A compass clear, through doubt and fear.
For character, though soft in tone,
Carries the weight of worlds alone.

51

As You Do Anything

A surgeon's hand, so steady, still,
Reflects the mind, the sharpened will.
For in the small, the soul is seen,
A mirror polished, sharp, and keen.

Each stitch, each thought, each whispered thread,
Reveals the paths our spirits tread.
From patient care to fleeting chores,
Our essence spills through every pore.

For no great feat is born alone,
In every act, a seed is sown.
The grains of sand build mountains high,
As countless stars light up the sky.

Vedanta whispers: every task,
Is life's unspoken, sacred ask.
Approach with care, as though divine,
For even the mundane holds a shrine.

Thus, heed the truth: in all you do,
The self you build reflects the you.
For every step, each fleeting thing,
Defines the tune your soul will sing.

52

The Subtle Imprint

Every action leaves a trace,
A silent mark, a fleeting face.
The words we choose, the thoughts we keep,
Carve furrows deep, though minds may sleep.

The brain, it wires through what we choose,
In patterns clear, or tangled ruse.
Neurons fire, connections mend,
Our habits shape the paths they send.

The Gita speaks of karma's thread,
Of acts unspoken, yet widely spread.
For what we sow, though we may part,
Returns to knock on every heart.

Character grows through small details,
In quiet strength, where patience sails.
It's not the storms we rise above,
But steady grace, and acts of love.

So, tend each moment, trim the vine,
And let your thoughts and deeds align.
For who you are, though hidden now,
Will bloom when time allows its bough.

53

A House of Sand or Stone

A castle built on shifting sand,
Will never hold, nor ever stand.
But stones, though plain, when stacked with care,
Withstand the storm, the fiercest air.

Our character is such a home,
A sacred place where hearts may roam.
Each lie a crack, each truth a beam,
Each act a thread within the seam.

The sages spoke of dharma's way,
A path of strength, though skies turn gray.
For doing right, though none may see,
Is how the soul finds clarity.

Even science lends its voice,
Behavior builds the neural choice.
As structures form, the self unfolds,
In patterns true or ones that mold.

Build wisely, then, with heart and hand,
A house that on firm truth may stand.
For what you build, though years may fade,
Will shelter all the self has made.

54

The Small Is the Great

It's not the grand, the bold, the loud,
But tiny acts that lift the crowd.
The unseen deeds, the humble way,
That shape the night and build the day.

The quiet scholar, buried deep,
In books that few would choose to keep,
May light a torch for years to come,
A silent hymn, a steady drum.

The Upanishads whisper softly still,
Greatness lies in quiet will.
For as the ocean drinks each stream,
The vast is fed by what may seem.

The brain, too, thrives on minor things,
Small sparks that build its endless rings.
Each habit, thought, or gesture mild,
Transforms the mind, reshapes the wild.

So tend the small, the fleeting task,
And watch its fruits in brilliance bask.
For as you do the smallest chore,
You shape the self forevermore.

55

The Favor of Time

Time's favor flows like a quantum stream,
Folding and bending the edges of a dream.
A particle paused, a wave that lingers,
Tracing eternity with unseen fingers.

Each delay, a cosmic choreography spins,
Orbits of patience where wisdom begins.
What the eye calls stillness, the soul perceives,
A symphony of moments the universe weaves.

The pendulum swings, yet the hands don't race,
For even in waiting, there's infinite grace.
Each second unfurls like a star's distant light,
Traveling eons to dazzle the night.

What seems like drift is alignment's art,
A celestial map drawn deep in the heart.
No detour wasted, no silence untrue,
Each curve of time is sculpting you.

56

The Fourth Dimension

Time—the veiled fourth, unseen but profound,
A silent dimension where destinies are bound.
Each moment delayed, a ripple in space,
An echo elsewhere, where futures embrace.

Who's to say if this pause is a cosmic refrain,
A prelude to actions in a parallel plane?
For every still second, another thread weaves,
In some distant metaverse, where life perceives.

Delays are not voids; they're portals unshown,
Where the seeds of tomorrow are quietly sown.
A pause here may bloom in the realm ahead,
What seems to falter could simply be led.

Attention bends time, as Einstein confessed,
Yet, could it be that the "now" is compressed?
A rest in this timeline, a step in the next,
The fabric of existence infinitely complexed.

So, fear not the stillness; it whispers design,
A blueprint celestial, a moment divine.
For time, like the stars, has no straight flight,
It curves and it dances, through shadow and light.

And thus, delays aren't a loss but a gift,
A recalibration, a metaphysical shift.
In the theater of dimensions, the script's never done,
Every pause in the present births galaxies to come.

57

The Masquerade of Coping Mechanisms

We all wear masks to hide the cracks,
In fragile hearts and weathered tracks.
A shield of "defensive pride," a boastful gleam,
Concealing wounds, a hidden theme.

Through "over-intellectualization," we quell the storm,
Reason replaces the heart's true form.
Loss dissected, emotions denied,
Yet emptiness grows where feelings reside.

With "projection's lens," we shift the blame,
Reflecting fears with another's name.
A clever trick to guard our soul,
But healing demands we claim control.

In "compartments," we place our pain aside,
Living as if two worlds collide.
Warmth at home, yet work turns cold,
Fragmented hearts too heavy to hold.

"Displacement" strikes, emotions stray,
Anger finds a safer way.

Yet misplaced wrath will always burn,
A lesson ignored, a cycle unturned.

"Humor" steps in, the jester's flair,
Hiding wounds too deep to bear.
A laugh, a quip, a jest so light,
But unspoken truths still haunt the night.

"Perfectionism" whispers its constant call,
To fix, refine, and fear the fall.
But in the quest for flawless grace,
We lose ourselves in a ceaseless race.

Through "avoidance," we turn away,
From fears and truths we'll face "someday."
But problems grow in shadows cast,
And haunt us more when time has passed.

The "people-pleaser" gives and bends,
Seeking approval, losing friends.
Boundaries blur, exhaustion reigns,
Kindness unreturned leaves hidden pains.

"Rationalization" smooths the tale,
Excuses mask where efforts fail.
Blame the world, deny the cost,
Yet growth remains forever lost.

"Self-sabotage," the quiet thief,
Feeds on doubt and disbelief.

Dreams undone by our own hand,
A future lost to fears unplanned.

"Fantasy" paints a perfect hue,
Escaping life for skies of blue.
Yet castles built on clouds so high,
Fall apart when storms draw nigh.

Each mask we wear, a silent plea,
To hide the pain, to seem carefree.
But in unveiling, our truth begins,
For healing blooms when we let it in.

58

Portraits of Personality

In the gallery of minds, where we all reside,
Each frame unique, no need to hide.
The Extrovert, a blazing sun,
Thrives on chatter, life's a fun run.

The Introvert, a quiet stream,
Finds peace in thought, a private dream.
Ambiverts dance, where worlds align,
Balancing loud and silent signs.

The Conscientious, steadfast and true,
Plans the journey, sees it through.
While the Open, curious and bright,
Embraces change, seeks new light.

The Agreeable, with warmth and care,
Spreads harmony, beyond compare.
And the Neurotic, a tempest inside,
Seeks calm but wrestles the rising tide.

These traits we hold, a wondrous blend,
Together they shape how lives transcend.

59

The Crossroads of Response

A fork in the road, a choice to make,
How do we respond, what path to take?

Fight, the flame that burns so bold,
Defends the self, the strong, the cold.
Flight, the wind that sweeps away,
Avoids the threat, finds another day.

Freeze, a shadow, paralyzed in fear,
Caught in the moment, danger near.
And Fawn, the bow of appeasement's art,
Seeks to please with a trembling heart.

But when Reason joins the fray,
Choices clear the foggy way.
The mind decides how best to stand,
To face life's trials with a steady hand.

60

The Abyss of Depression

A weight descends, unseen, profound,
A silent scream, no echoed sound.
In shadows thick, where sunlight wanes,
The heart is heavy, tethered in chains.

Hobbies fade, a dimming hue,
What once brought joy feels distant, too.
Sleep evades or grips too tight,
Both day and night blur into night.

The mind whispers, "You're all alone,"
Yet help resides, a call, a tone.
Therapy's light, a guiding flame,
Medication may soothe what words can't name.

Depression's storm, though fierce it seems,
Can lift with care, restoring dreams.

61

《Superconscious Compartmentalization》

The path to triumph, every quandary's key,
Lies in the mind's deliberate decree.
To carve the hours, a sovereign task assign,
And let each moment with precision shine.

Through Karma Yoga's flow, with zeal imbued,
Each block of time its sacred purpose renewed.
Within that span, no thought shall stray nor wane,
But steadfast action, unalloyed by vain.

Zen mindfulness holds past and future at bay,
Its tranquil poise guides the present's foray.
Through undivided focus, the self transcends,
And mastery blooms as awareness ascends.

With Stoic resolve, let the hours refine,
Each moment etched by an unwavering line.
Superconscious will, through segments aligned,
Unlocks success, by thought and time combined.

62

In Quietitude:

Let Thy Come to Thee

Success in life, a butterfly fair,
That flees thy grasp and mocks thy care.
Thy hands outstretched, it flits away,
Yet stillness bids it soft to stay.

In flow's embrace, where time doth fade,
Thy craft is honed, thy peace is made.
The least of paths, the quietest stream,
Doth guide thee close to thy heart's dream.

From ancient truths, this wisdom's spun:
Desires fall off when thou art one.
Rest in thy Self, where stillness reigns,
And bliss descends, like gentle rains.

From timeless lore, let duty lead,
Detach from fruits, nor bow to greed.
For when thou dost in effort abide,
The butterfly rests by thy side.

63

The Power of Duty, Detached from Results

In the field of life, we toil with grace,
Without the promise of any embrace.
We sow the seeds, though none we see,
For harvest's joy is not for me.

Our hands, though calloused, move in tune,
To the rhythm of a silent boon.
The duty calls, not for the gain,
But for the purity we obtain.

Let go of fruit, let go of greed,
For in the labor, we find the seed.
Detached from hope, yet firm we stand,
Guided by a higher hand.

64

The Belief That Shapes the Self

What you believe, that you become,
The mind, a canvas, blank and numb.
Each thought a stroke, each wish a hue,
Shaping the world as if it's true.

A dream is real, if you dare to see,
What was once a shadow, now flies free.
The mind, a mirror to the heart's refrain,
Reflects our truths, our joys, our pain.

So shape your thoughts with gentle care,
For they craft the life you will wear.
Believe in light, and it will shine,
For what you hold becomes divine.

65

The Mind - Best Friend or Worst Enemy

The mind, a beast with fire in its eyes,
Tears at the soul with unseen ties.
But tamed and led, it sings a tune,
Of peace and joy beneath the moon.

It whispers fears, it calls for doubt,
A shadow's dance, a scream, a shout.
Yet those who master this wild voice,
Find calm within, their heart's own choice.

A friend, a guide, a loyal steed,
The mind, when tamed, fulfills the need.
To conquer self is to find the key,
And make the mind your sanctuary.

66

The Delusion of Anger

In anger's grasp, the world turns gray,
What once was clear now fades away.
A fire burns, it blinds the eyes,
And clouds the truth with bitter lies.

In rage, the heart becomes a storm,
The mind a twisted, warped form.
And what was once a path of light,
Now lost in shadows, veiled in night.

But in the calm, the truth is found,
Beyond the anger, there's solid ground.
Release the flame, and stillness reigns,
For peace returns when anger wanes.

67

The Sacredness of Self-Action

Every task is sacred when done with grace,
A sacrifice, a peaceful space.
In every step, the divine resides,
In every action, the universe abides.

No longer driven by need or greed,
We act with love, we act with speed.
For in the sacrifice, we are set free,
Bound to no one, just the eternal sea.

The work we do is not for gain,
But for the world to feel the reign.
Of love, of light, of truth, of peace,
In every task, our hearts release.

68

The Mirror of Self

The greatest foe lies within the chest,
A mirror cracked, a mind distressed.
A friend, too, in the depths resides,
A guide that in the heart confides.

The battle rages, unseen, unfelt,
Between the self, where feelings melt.
But harmony lies in self-control,
To make the mind and heart whole.

So, seek the friend, not the foe,
And in your soul, let peace flow.
For in the heart, where truth resides,
Self becomes the guide that never hides.

69

The Eternal Dance of Life and Death

In the dance of time, I lead the way,
The start, the middle, the end of the day.
I am the breath, the rise, the fall,
The first, the last, I am all.

From dust to dust, the journey flows,
Through endless cycles, it goes and goes.
I am the spark that ignites the flame,
I am the end, the timeless name.

Embrace the change, for it is me,
I am the truth, the life, the sea.
In every moment, I am here,
The beginning, the middle, the end, so near.

70

The Timeless Essence

Fear not, O soul, if you fall,
For in your steps, you stand tall.
Each movement, each breath, each tear,
Is a lesson, drawing you near.

No effort wasted, no action in vain,
For even struggle breaks the chain.
The journey leads, step by step,
To wisdom, truth, and peace adept.

In every failure, strength is born,
In every trial, we are reborn.
Nothing is lost, nothing is wrong,
For in your heart, you belong.

71

The Path of Self-Discovery

The path is long, a winding trail,
Where doubts arise and footsteps fail.
Yet in your heart, a flame is sown,
A quiet truth, unseen but known.

Through shadows deep, the soul must go,
Where fears dissolve and wisdom flows.
Each question asked, a seed of light,
To break the veil and clear your sight.

The storms will test, the winds will call,
But rise again when you may fall.
For in each step, the self unfolds,
A story written, a truth retold.

So walk with faith, though dim the way,
Let courage be your guide and stay.
The journey ends where it began,
Within your soul, the timeless plan.

72

The Courage to Let Go

Let go of what binds, let go of the chains,
Of the past's grip, and the future's reigns.
In the present moment, stand and breathe,
Release the mind, let the heart believe.

No need to clutch, no need to hold,
For what's meant for you will unfold.
Let go, and you shall find the peace,
That waits within, where struggles cease.

In letting go, the soul is free,
A bird that soars, eternally.
Trust the flow, let the river run,
For in release, we become one.

73

The Invisible Force of Faith

Faith is the ember in twilight's chest,
A whisper that stirs when all else rests.
It dances unseen, where reason fails,
A phantom breeze in forgotten trails.

It holds the keel when tempests roar,
A compass carved on the soul's dark shore.
Through tangled woods where light withdraws,
Faith threads the path with silent laws.

When doubt casts shadows on weary minds,
It moves like roots through broken binds.
An unseen hand, both firm and slight,
That steadies the heart in endless night.

So, trust its pulse, though veiled and thin,
For faith ignites the fire within.
It bends the dark to shape the dawn,
A force unseen, yet ever strong.

74

The Power of Acceptance

Acceptance is the key, the door,
That opens up to what's in store.
To surrender to life's flow,
And let the current carry us below.

Resisting is but a heavy chain,
That locks us in eternal pain.
But when we let go and simply be,
The world becomes a symphony.

Acceptance does not mean defeat,
But understanding life's heartbeat.
It's in the flow, the ease, the grace,
Where we find our rightful place.

75

Beyond the Surface

Beyond the skin, beyond the face,
Lies a world of boundless space.
We are not what others see,
But the essence of what we choose to be.

The soul, the mind, the heart's deep core,
Is a realm of peace, forevermore.
So don't be swayed by outward guise,
For true beauty is in the skies.

Look within, and there you'll find,
The truth that transcends, forever kind.
Beyond the surface, beyond the mask,
Lie all the answers, if you dare to ask.

76

The Strength in Silence

Silence speaks louder than words could tell,
In its quietude, the soul does dwell.
It's the pause between each thought,
The peace in which we are truly caught.

In the stillness, strength is born,
A quiet power, not worn or torn.
It's the breath that calms the storm,
The space that makes the heart transform.

So, embrace the silence, let it be,
A place where you are truly free.
In the stillness, we are whole,
A gentle peace within the soul.

77

The Gift of Resilience

Resilience is the heart that bends,
But never breaks, it always mends.
Through every storm, it finds its way,
And rises stronger every day.

It's the fire that burns through the night,
A spark of hope, a guiding light.
Though bruised and battered, it stands tall,
For resilience rises after the fall.

In every hardship, there's a seed,
Of strength, of growth, of love indeed.
So wear resilience like your skin,
For through it, all victories begin.

78

The Journey of Self-Love

To love yourself is not a task,
But a journey you needn't ask.
It's the way you speak, the way you care,
The love you give, the love you share.

In every flaw, in every tear,
Love finds its place, without fear.
For the heart is vast, the soul is wide,
In self-love, you cannot hide.

So embrace yourself with open arms,
And let go of all past harms.
For in the mirror, you'll see the truth,
That love begins with you, in youth.

79

The Strength of Forgiveness

Forgiveness is the quiet key,
That unlocks the chains of memory.
It softens wounds that time won't mend,
And bids the fractured heart to bend.

It is no surrender, no fading fight,
But the soul's release to endless light.
A balm unseen, a whispering grace,
That clears the shadows we cannot face.

To forgive is to loosen the silent weight,
To rewrite pain, to reshape fate.
Let anger dissolve, let hatred decay,
And find your freedom in love's pure sway.

For forgiveness is the path we tread,
Where heavy hearts grow light instead.
It carves the road to peaceful streams,
And brighter nights where the spirit dreams.

80

The Journey of Transformation

Transformation is a silent art,
A shift within the human heart.
From darkness to light, from loss to gain,
Through every tear, through every pain.

It's the butterfly that takes to flight,
A change unseen, but full of light.
The soul evolves, the mind anew,
A never-ending journey through and through.

So, trust the process, trust the change,
For growth happens, though it feels strange.
Transformation, deep and true,
Is the path that leads to you.

81

The Wisdom of Stillness

Stillness is a gift, a balm for the soul,
A place of peace where we become whole.
In the quiet, the answers lie,
To questions unspoken, to the why.

It's in the pause, the breath, the wait,
Where wisdom comes, where we relate.
No rush, no hurry, no need to flee,
For stillness brings the mind to see.

In silence, truth reveals its face,
A timeless wisdom, a gentle grace.
So seek the stillness, find your way,
In quietude, the world will stay.

82

The Equation of Life

Action is ours, a force in play,
The outcome, a variable swept away.
A catalyst ignites what we start,
But the system evolves, each part its part.

Choices form the initial spark,
Yet chaos rules where light meets dark.
Circumstances ripple, unseen, unplanned,
Shaping results with a steady hand.

What seems a loss, a failed design,
May lead to breakthroughs yet to align.
The weight that drags, the storm that bends,
Often creates the shape that mends.

For those who harm, those who guide,
Are vectors in equations wide.
Our limits see but fragments near,
While destiny writes what's far and clear.

Errors, triumphs, all interweave,
Formulas beyond what minds conceive.
What hurts today may teach tomorrow,
From heat and pressure, diamonds borrow.

Embrace the flow, let go of strife,
Each reaction births new life.
When outcomes break, it's not the end,
But energy moving, a curve to bend.

Gratitude turns chaos to peace,
Uncertainty births the masterpiece.
Control's illusion, our part to play,
The experiment runs, come what may.

83

When Faults Disguise as Virtues

A man who thinks his faults are skills,
Adorns his crown with gilded ills.
The cunning mind, a web does weave,
Believing guile will never leave.

The greedy call their lust ambition,
A hunger masked by keen precision.
The liar crafts his world of art,
A truthless tale to win a heart.

The arrogant, with haughty air,
Deems himself beyond compare.
Aggression dons a leader's guise,
While harm is done beneath disguise.

Manipulation's tender hand,
Rebrands deceit as something grand.
The conspirator, with whispered schemes,
Views his shadows as bright beams.

A gossiper, with silver tongue,
Believes connections thus are sung.
Reckless thrill, the risk-taker's creed,

Mistakes boldness for reckless speed.

Perfection blinds with gilded sheen,
A fruitless chase for what has been.
The stubborn fool, steadfast in plight,
Deems folly as a mark of might.

Pause, and let your heart reflect,
On deeds you hold in high respect.
For cunning fades, and greed shall rust,
And truth, alone, deserves your trust.

Seek wisdom's light, and not the flare,
Of fleeting praise or hollow care.
For life is not the game you play,
But what you build along the way.

84

Meandering Time's Non-Linear Tapestry

Time, a dimension unbound by decay,
Where entropy whispers, yet doesn't betray.
Simultaneity folds within the quanta's glide,
Moments converge, where all truths reside.

Cosmic cycles spin in infinite recursion,
A fractal dance, defying progression.
Creation and collapse, intertwined and whole,
In spacetime's fabric, we find the soul.

Parallel births, where all lifetimes unite,
Exist at once, beyond the limits of sight.
Superposed selves in an endless array,
We live all futures, pasts, and today.

Each action a waveform, collapsing to choice,
In the field of existence, we find our voice.
Parallel paths diverge, converge, align,
A lattice of outcomes in the continuum of time.

So transcend the linear, embrace the profound,
In quantum oscillations, we're eternally bound.
For in the illusion of separation's guise,
The universe unfolds within your eyes.

85

Postman of Thy Fate

When fate decides, it sends its call,
Through messengers, who stand quite tall.
Yet blame them not for what they bring,
For they control not anything.

A letter sealed with destiny's thread,
Delivered straight, no words unsaid.
But they are merely hands of fate,
Not ones to judge or speculate.

The storm may rise, the winds may blow,
But peace remains in what we know.
For all we face, we're meant to see,
No one to blame but destiny.

Don't give them power, don't let them win,
They weren't capable, it wasn't their spin.
Just postmen playing their destined part,
They carried the message, not the heart.

So as you stand, don't curse or cry,
The postman's role is to comply.
The journey's ours, the lesson too,
Accept the path that's given to you.

86

¡Renunciation!

A war unfolds within the silent mind,
Its restless gusts like whispers undefined.
For some, a maelstrom, fierce and bold,
A tempest tearing through the soul's stronghold.

The thoughts careen, unbridled, far and wide,
Sweeping through the chambers where we hide.
Like winds that shift and scatter, swift and blind,
Their aimless course leaves clarity behind.

Yet deep within, a truth begins to bloom:
No force can quell the mind's relentless fume.
With steady practice, discipline refined,
The wayward winds grow tame, the heart aligned.

Renunciation—sweet, untethered grace—
Loosens the chains of longing's fierce embrace.
To scorn what's fleeting, transient in our sight,
Is to unearth the soul's most gentle light.

Through abhyāsa, patient hands will mold
The scattered sands into a form of gold.
Detachment, soft as twilight's fall, will steer
The mind to stillness, crystalline and clear.

No longer tossed by every gale or gust,

We find in letting go, a deeper trust.
For in release, true mastery is known—
In renunciation, the self is shown.

87

Cosmic Rhythms: The Dance of Fate and Fortune

In the dance of fate, where quarks align,
Hard work's the spark, but time's the spine.
Luck, the unseen force, in orbits does it twine,
A cosmic play, where stars refine.

In Vedic lore and physics' wave,
Karma's thread and entropic stave.
A quantum leap, in life's grand nave,
God scripts our path, when tides behave.

For even when with effort you persist,
Chaos and chance can't be dismissed.
Like Schrödinger's cat in paradoxes exist,
Only divine will can truth enlist.

So toil with heart, but gaze above,
The universe shifts in rhythms of love.
When fortune turns, and heavens shove,
It's then you'll find, what you're worthy of.

88

Entropic Embrace: Love's Chaotic Symphony

In love's thermodynamics, a subtle interplay,
Entropic affections, in chaos they may sway.
Calorific passions, a heat that consumes,
Yet entropy lurks, as romance booms.

A phase transition, love's metamorphosis,
Solid foundations, in the warmth we reminisce.
Molecular bonds, binding hearts in collusion,
Yet beware, for entropy breeds confusion.

In the dance of hearts, entropy may play its part,
Yet the alchemy of love, a resilient art.
A paradigm where disorder finds its rhyme,
In the entropy of love, transcending space and time.

Entropy's decree, as relationships unfold,
Heat dissipates, like stories untold.
In this love thermodynamic, where chaos aligns,
The equilibrium of hearts be the sweetest signs.

As the year concludes, in a poetic veneer,
Wishing all a new year, love-laden and clear.
May the entropy of joy defy the norm,
Happy New Year, where love takes its form.

89

Harmony of Resilience: Cosmic Cadence in Life's Classroom

In life's grand classroom, where patience unfolds,
I've learned to combat, to seize what life holds.
A symphony of questions, in balance they sway,
Yet in my faith, God's trust lights my way.

With each redirection, a punch from time's hand,
Motivation surges, a resilient stand.
To love, to ponder, in moments profound,
Every setback a chance, wisdom to expound.

In the ring of trials, where disappointments may gleam,
I yearn for victories, an elusive dream.
Yet within each defeat, hope tightly coiled,
A belief that the sun, brighter, is foiled.

Life's lessons, a dance, as the stars are aligned,
Philosophical whispers, in corridors of the mind.
Scientific symphonies, theories intertwine,
A cosmic ballet, where destinies entwine.

So, let the rhythm of life play its tune,
In the vast expanse, beneath the waning moon.
For in the echoes of struggle, a resilient theme,
I find the essence of life, a glamorous dream.

90

?Uncertainty?

Amidst the mystic quest for swiftness in flight,
Perception of position dissolves in twilight.
Uncertainty's veil, a cloak of cosmic lace,
In Heisenberg's whispers, reality we embrace.

In quantum realms, where particles entwine,
Heisenberg's enigma, a puzzle divine.
Certainty eludes, like grains of shifting sand,
Reality's brush strokes painted by an unseen hand.

Yet transcending equations, logic's embrace,
Life pirouettes, a waltz full of grace.
Illusions of mastery, in truth's soft light,
Life commandeers, the captain of the night.

In the labyrinth of existence, we dwell,
Fate's intricate tapestry, a story to tell.
Threads of chance and choice interlace,
As life weaves patterns only time can erase.

Amidst uncertainty's embrace, we bloom,
In shadows and whispers, we find our room.
Destiny's kaleidoscope, vivid and fleet,
Life's mystery profound, both bitter and sweet.

91

Shout is a Hidden Cry

The waspish lion and its roar,
The tetchy storm and the sound at shore,
The splenetic clouds and the sound of thunder,
Do they all mean power, let's ponder!

The loudness of voice and the fiery expressions,
The outrage or the burst of emotions
Is it a way to show the brawn?
Or a way to hide the inner squall?

The statements with substance don't need a noise
The voice is enough, and expression is just a choice
Only the drowning noob pushes it harder
It's the sense of fear and weakness that entices extra
power!

The Shout is a Hidden Cry
Telling the tale of a journey astray
'Displacement' of the emotions missed
& frustrations of the irate man to fulfill his wish
Don't get angry against the shout
Try to feel the cry and the drought
Offer to help and hug the heart
The better world, lets give it a start!

92.

The Silent Storm

A storm may rage, but not in sight,
It brews within, hidden from light.
The clouds may darken, the winds may scream,
But no one sees the silent dream.

It's not the thunder, nor the rain,
But the quiet that holds the strain.
A soul may twist, a heart may break,
But it's the silence that aches, not fake.

In the stillness, the storm will roar,
No need for noise, it seeks no more.
The calm it wears, the peace it craves,
Are only found in quiet waves.

So when you see the storm inside,
Don't fear the silence where it hides.
For in the quiet, strength is born,
The storm is calm, the heart reborn.

93

The Hidden Fire

A fire burns within the chest,
It heats the soul, it never rests.
But no one sees the flames that rise,
Hidden beneath the calm disguise.

The fire's quiet, soft, and bright,
A burning glow in the dead of night.
It may not roar, it may not scream,
But in the heart, it starts to gleam.

The quiet flame is just as strong,
A steady glow, the soul's sweet song.
It doesn't need the blaze or smoke,
It speaks in silence, never broke.

So when you feel the fire inside,
Don't fear the quiet, don't try to hide.
For in the stillness, strength will show,
The fire that continues to grow.

94

The Soul's Journey

The soul, unshackled, drifts through time,
A transient spark, a flame sublime.
Through realms it roams, untouched by night,
Beyond the veil of earthly sight.

In bodies cast, it knows no end,
Each life a journey, each step to mend.
The heart, a vessel, seeks the way,
Through samsara's dance, it learns to sway.

Eternal, it moves, yet still it stands,
The truth it seeks with gentle hands.
Like wind that whispers through the trees,
It finds its peace in endless seas.

For in its depths, the Atman shines,
A flame eternal, none can bind.
It seeks not form, nor fleeting glow,
For it is all, and all it knows.

95

The Silent Truth

The self, elusive, hides from view,
Beneath the layers, pure and true.
No eye can see, nor mind can grasp,
The truth concealed within its clasp.

Through quietude, the truth is found,
Not in the noise, but in the sound
Of stillness deep, where all is one,
Where time and space are both undone.

In every breath, the self does speak,
A subtle voice, both soft and meek.
Yet in its words, the cosmos turns,
A light that in the darkness burns.

The Atman whispers through the air,
A secret shared in timeless prayer.
And when the seeker stops to listen,
The world itself begins to glisten.

96

Beyond the Illusion

The world is but a fleeting dream,
A shadow in a moonlit beam.
What seems so real, so firm, so true,
Is naught but a mirage in view.

Behind the veil, a light does gleam,
The essence pure, the soul's bright beam.
It shines within, it shines without,
A truth unspoken, beyond doubt.

Through layers thick, the heart must pierce,
To see the world in its true sphere.
Beyond the form, beyond the mind,
A sacred truth awaits to find.

So let the illusion fade away,
And let the self in stillness sway.
For in the silence, we shall see,
The oneness of eternity.

97

The Hidden Self

Hidden within, the self does lie,
Beyond the clouds, beyond the sky.
No outward form can it betray,
For it is the stillness of the day.

It is not flesh, nor bone, nor breath,
It is the light that conquers death.
It cannot speak, nor be confined,
It lives within the heart and mind.

Through meditation, deep and pure,
The self reveals its essence sure.
In silence vast, the truth unfurls,
And the soul becomes the infinite whirl.

The ego fades, the self remains,
A silent force that breaks all chains.
And in that peace, the soul will find,
Its place within the heart of time.

98

■ Nothing is Absolute ■

Nothing is absolute—no verity endures the tide.
Science, audacious and unmoored, scales reason's
mountainside.
Hindu dharma, vast as aeons, extols the paradox
arcane,
Conceding that all fixed truths may shatter and wane.

What stands as doctrine in the morn, by dusk may
disband,
For wisdom flows in mutable streams through
fleeting sands.
Dimensions warp; axioms fray; no edict withstands,
The cosmos etches riddles deep with unseen, shifting
hands.

Liberty fuels the seeker's spark—untethered by
decree,
To fathom, to traverse, to savor truths in boundless
spree.
Pragmatic trails and ruminant thoughts in sacred
cadence meet,
Finite minds breach infinite gates, where mysteries
entreat.

In kalpa's churn and quantum's wisp, the ephemeral
truth lies,
Each frame a glimmer of the grand concealed in
cosmic skies.
Maya's veil and reason's flame, both deify the quest,
For nothing remains immutable; flux itself is best.

Oh paradox, thy solemn psalm—an aegis in the haze,
To challenge what is deemed as law, yet ever onward
blaze.
The vast abyss, a boundless call, invites the soul to
roam,
For nothing is absolute—yet in this flux, we're home.

99

The Hidden Light

A light is hidden in the dark,
The soul's pure flame, the heart's true spark.
It flickers soft, it glows so bright,
Yet only in the dark of night.

In stillness deep, the soul is found,
It moves beyond the outer sound.
The mind, a mirror, reflects the view,
But the self is always born anew.

It burns within, a flame untold,
A force of love, a truth of gold.
Through ages past, through time unknown,
The self stands constant, all alone.

And in this light, we find our way,
Beyond the dawn, beyond the day.
For in the dark, the soul does see,
The hidden light that sets us free.

100

Infinite Ocean

The ocean vast, the depths untold,
The self within, the truth so bold.
It stretches wide, it moves through time,
In waves that rise, in waves that climb.

In every drop, the ocean's grace,
A boundless truth, a sacred place.
The self within, a drop in all,
Yet in its heart, the universe calls.

Through every wave, through every storm,
The soul remains in perfect form.
No matter where, no matter when,
The ocean's peace will come again.

For in the depths, the truth we find,
A love unbroken, pure, and kind.
The self is ocean, vast and free,
The boundless truth of you and me.

101

The Silent Path

The path is silent, still, and clear,
The way is known to those who hear.
In every step, the truth is near,
In every breath, it does appear.

No need to speak, no need to shout,
The path is found within, no doubt.
The soul does walk, yet never moves,
It is the stillness that it proves.

Through every trial, through every test,
The self remains, forever blessed.
For in the silence, peace does grow,
And in that peace, the soul does flow.

So let the world pass by in haste,
In silence pure, we find our place.
For in the quiet, we will see,
The endless truth that sets us free.

102

The One Within

(The Key to Discipline and Conscious Mastery)

Within the self, the universe wide,
The answer's not in the world outside.
No distant quest, no force afar,
The key to truth lies where we are.

It's not in searching the outer sky,
But in the stillness where we lie.
The power to heal, the strength to rise,
Lies within, beyond disguise.

Through self-control, through mindful grace,
We awaken the soul in sacred space.
In discipline, the self refines,
Unlocking the power, where truth aligns.

The chakras rise, a silent flame,
Each center bright, no longer tame.
From root to crown, the energy flows,
A force within that only grows.

The path to mastery is drawn within,
A journey of balance, where it begins.
Through control of mind, through mastery deep,
We awaken the truths that lie asleep.

No outer force, no fleeting trend,
Can heal the soul, can help it mend.
The power lies within the heart,
The conscious prime, where we start.

In every thought, in every breath,
The self transcends all life and death.
By stilling the mind, by calming the storm,
We reach our soul's highest form.

So let us rise, let us begin,
To conquer ourselves, to truly win.
For in the self, the truth is clear,
The key to peace, the end of fear.

103

The Unfolding Cosmos

Before time's first whisper, there was silence —
A void untouched, a space of stillness,
Yet in that quiet, all things found existence,
A truth unspoken, yet full of persistence.

The sages did not view the world as separate,
But as a reflection, a mind's deep narrative.
Their teachings spoke of laws unseen,
Invisible forces shaping all that's been.

Now science peels back the fabric of space,
Revealing the particles that dance in place.
Each governed by forces beyond our sight,
A universe born of both dark and light.

In the quantum realm, where certainty fades,
We seek the meaning in ancient shades.
Matter and thought, both formed from one,
A truth that's endless, a race never run.

The stars, once guides to those on the sea,
Now whisper secrets of what's meant to be.
No contradiction lies in their ancient glow —
Both wisdom and science, together they flow.

At the crossroads of reason and faith, we stand,
Where intellect and instinct hold hand in hand.
The universe is both thought and form,
A truth unyielding, both calm and warm.

104

The Dream of Life

Life is but a fleeting dream,
A flicker in a cosmic stream.
What seems so real, what seems so true,
Is but a shadow passing through.

Behind the veil, the truth is bright,
A flame that burns in endless light.
The dream fades, the self remains,
Untouched by time, untouched by chains.

In every dream, the self does play,
In every form, it finds its way.
No end, no start, no boundary wide,
The self, eternal, cannot hide.

So let us live, but not in fear,
The dream is here, the truth is clear.
For in the self, we come to know,
The endless truth that makes us whole.

105

The Infinite Peace

Peace is the path, the soul's delight,
It is the dawn, the endless night.
In peace, the self begins to rise,
And sees the truth with opened eyes.

No war, no strife, no endless fight,
The peace of self is pure and bright.
It lies within, it lies beyond,
A light that beckons, soft and fond.

In peace, the heart does find its grace,
It sees the world as one embrace.
The self is peace, the peace is true,
It lives in all, it lives in you.

So let us walk the path of peace,
And from all fear and hate release.
For in the peace, we come to see,
The boundless truth that sets us free.

106

The Unity of All

In unity, all things are one,
The moon, the stars, the shining sun.
In every leaf, in every stone,
The soul's reflection, fully grown.

No separate form, no fractured line,
In unity, the truth we find.
All beings rise, all beings fall,
Yet in the soul, we transcend it all.

The self is all, the all is one,
No difference, no division, none.
In every heart, in every breath,
The soul persists, defying death.

So let us see the truth in all,
The moon, the earth, the sky so tall.
For in the unity, we realize,
The boundless peace that never dies.

In this oneness, all is clear,
The sacred truth is drawing near.
For in the soul, we understand,
The unity of life's grand plan.

107

The Still Waters

Still waters reflect the boundless sky,
The soul within, where truths lie.
No ripple stirs, no wave does rise,
The superconscious mirrors the skies.

In silence deep, the self remains,
A steady mind where clarity reigns.
It reveals the whole, it shows the truth,
The heart, the soul, eternal and smooth.

Through all the world, the waters flow,
A love that shines, an endless glow.
No wave can shift, no storm can break,
The superconscious stands, for truth's own sake.

So let us sit where waters lie,
And witness truth, beyond the sky.
For in the stillness, we shall see,
The soul's reflection, wild and free.

In this calm, the mind expands,
A mirror clear, with no demands.
Awake within, the self ascends,
The superconscious, where all blends.

108

The Superconscious Awakening

Within the mind, a silent spark,
A flicker of truth within the dark.
Beyond the noise, beyond the strain,
Lies a state where we transcend the mundane.

The difference between success and fall,
Greatness and mediocrity — it's all,
In reaching the self that knows no bounds,
Where wisdom and clarity resound.

In the superconscious, we awake,
To the truths that we must undertake.
Active, present, with open eyes,
We see through the veil of our disguise.

To observe, to correct, with honest grace,
Not bound by time, but in a higher space.
This is the realm where greatness begins,
Where victory starts from within.

It's the courage to confront what's wrong,
To adjust, to evolve, to stay strong.

For in this state, we transcend the norm,
And rise above in the highest form.

Though easier said than done, we see,
The power within to set us free.
Awakened minds break through the haze,
Creating paths where others graze.

So, rise to your superconscious light,
Where clarity lives, and all feels right.
For in this state, success is born,
And greatness shines in every dawn.

.

Epilogue

The journey through *The VigyaVed Superconsciousness* does not end with the final poem, for the exploration of consciousness is an ongoing, eternal pursuit. What we have encountered in these verses is but a glimpse of the boundless realms of awareness that await discovery. Like the ancient sages who sought to understand the nature of existence, we, too, are on a path that leads us beyond the limits of time, space, and form.

As we move through the world, we are often distracted by the noise of our daily lives — the superficial pursuits of wealth, success, and recognition. But true understanding comes not from these external markers, but from turning inward, from looking deeply into the nature of the self. The superconscious mind is always with us, waiting to be awakened.

The number 108, which has guided this collection, is no mere number; it carries profound significance both scientifically and spiritually. In ancient texts, 108 is regarded as a sacred and auspicious number in Hinduism, Buddhism, and other spiritual traditions. It symbolizes the connection between the physical and spiritual realms, bridging the finite and the infinite. In the context of meditation, 108 beads on a mala are traditionally used to count the recitations of a mantra, embodying the cyclical nature of existence, a microcosmic reflection of the universe's vastness.

From a scientific perspective, 108 holds special relevance in several disciplines. For instance, the relationship between the sun, the earth, and the moon — a cosmic triad — is astonishingly linked to this number. The diameter of the Sun is approximately 108 times that of the Earth, and the distance between the Earth and the Sun is about 108 times the Sun's diameter. Similarly, the moon's diameter is about 108 times smaller than the Sun's. This convergence of numbers in the physical universe mirrors the harmony and interconnectedness found in spiritual teachings, reinforcing the idea that the physical and metaphysical worlds are inseparably linked.

Mathematically, 108 is significant as well. It is a Harshad number, meaning it is divisible by the sum of its digits. It also finds a place in geometry, where it appears in the angles of polygons, further representing the harmony and balance that the number encapsulates. This alignment with mathematical symmetry is echoed in the structure of this book — where each poem, as a unit, contributes to a larger, more complete understanding of the superconscious state, much like the universe itself, which functions with a cosmic order that is often beyond our comprehension.

Thus, the 108 poems of this collection are not arbitrary; they serve as a symbolic and deliberate structure to mirror the vastness of the journey into consciousness. Just as 108 in spiritual traditions represents a full cycle of meditation, encompassing both inward and outward focus, these poems form a complete cycle of exploration — from the deepest scientific inquiries to the profound spiritual revelations. Together, they represent an intricate weaving of science, spirituality, and poetry, designed to guide the reader into a fuller understanding of the superconscious state.

May this book serve as a reminder that there is more to reality than meets the eye, that the true nature of consciousness is a mystery that we are all called to explore. The answers we seek are not out there in the world, but within us. As we continue our journey through life, let us strive to move closer to that superconscious state, where all limitations dissolve, and we experience the eternal truth of our being.

In the end, we are all but waves on the surface of a vast ocean, but within each of us is the depth of that infinite sea. May we always remember to dive deeper, to look beyond the surface, and to live from the vastness of the superconscious.

www.ingramcontent.com/pod-product-compliance
Lightning Source LLC
Chambersburg PA
CBHW061344160726
47995CB00001B/165